CW00732720

You are my Sunshine

a LITTLE BOOK
for SOMEONE SPECIAL

You Are My Sunshine

for all your gift books and gift stationery

First published in 2023 by Allsorted Ltd WD19 4BG U.K.

© Susanna Geoghegan Gift Publishing
Author: Helen Vaux
Illustrator: Sue Reeves
Cover and concept design: Milestone Creative
Contents design: WW Creative
ISBN: 9781915902146
Printed in China
10 9 8 7 6 5 4 3 2 1

Introduction

Did you know that everyone is someone's sunshine?
We might not always realise it, but each of us brings
joy into someone else's life and brightens up their day.
That's a wonderful gift. This little book of uplifting
quotes and affirmations celebrates the special
warmth and happiness we all have the power to
radiate. It reminds us how special we are, even when
our own skies sometimes feel grey.

Keep shining!

We can be our own worst enemies when it comes to recognising our positive qualities. It's easy to be too busy with work or life to stop and take a moment to appreciate how amazing we are. Today, take a moment to acknowledge any specific achievement that has made a difference to someone else. It's okay to feel proud of being a good person!

If I could give you one thing, it would be the ability to see yourself through my eyes. Only then you will truly understand

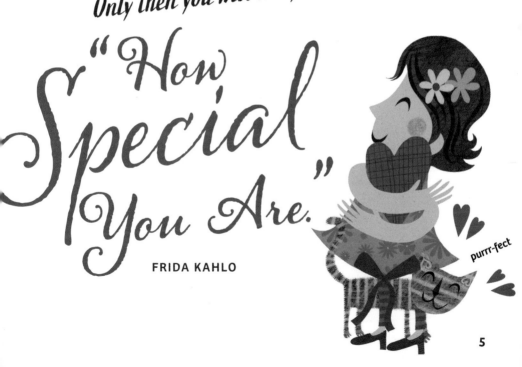

"How Special You Are."

FRIDA KAHLO

purrr-fect

"Brighten Up the Days"

when everything around feels dark.

What an incredible feeling it is to be able to bring a glow into someone's life. It's not even about doing something — sometimes just being there is all that's needed. We can't always fix other people's troubles, but being a comforting presence can help them see light and hope. And that means the people around us will never feel alone.

Whether it's for an extended period or simply until
the following day, saying 'Goodbye' to someone
who brings sunshine into our lives is hard. Rather
than feeling sad, embrace the anticipation of being
reunited with them in the future.

8

See You Soon

The pain of parting
is nothing to the

"Joy of Meeting
Again."

CHARLES DICKENS

"Be a Mirror."

Each of us can aspire to become a strong, guiding light through the smallest of words and actions. Individually, these may seem insignificant, but collectively, our support can light a path towards a better future. All it takes is for a few people to reflect one ray of sunshine – so let's start today!

Giving time and encouragement to others should never be a chore. When we do things for other people, we experience the greatest reward from knowing we have passed a lit baton to someone in need of light.

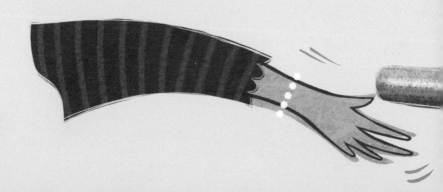

There are those who give
with joy, and that

"*Joy is Their Reward.*"

KHALIL GIBRAN

Joy

To the "Moon, the Stars & Back Again."

When someone compares their loved ones
to the stars and the solar system, they're not
exaggerating. These are objects which help us to
express a feeling that is bigger than words.
By taking these comparisons on board, we can
each become someone who means the world – or
more – to another human.

During life's challenging moments, it's good to
know we can rely on the support of others. Offering
unconditional love and words of advice can act as a
lifeline, so always try to be the person who is someone
else's tower of strength.

When I think of you, I think of kindness, wisdom and love.

"*Thanks For Being You.*"

SAM CROW

"Don't Forget to Breathe."

Life is full of challenges, and it's easy to forget to take a step back and breathe. Each of our positive attributes and achievements is a gift to the world and it's important to take a moment every now and then to remind ourselves of that. Take a deep breath, focus, and then start again.

Take a moment to bask in the glow of warm
feelings as they happen and live in the moment.
If we each spend a few seconds drinking in a perfect
sunset, or the scent of a perfect flower,
it will become second nature to seek out
something beautiful every day.

Keep your face to "The Sunshine" and you cannot see a shadow.

HELEN KELLER

Affirmations ... for

Self-Love

Self-love allows every individual to look out for their own emotional and mental well-being. Repeating these affirmations daily will act as a reminder about how amazing we all are.

- Today is a day to bring good things into the world.

- We are all worthy of good things.

- The brightest light follows the darkest times.

- Appreciate all the paths that open up before us.

- Love unconditionally.

- Reflect happiness and joy.

- I deserve happiness and joy.

- Positive things come to positive people.

- Remember: caring for others is part and parcel of caring for ourselves.

- Be open to new friendships.

- Don't apologise for being yourself.

Life is too short to worry about what other people think, and it's a waste of time trying to fit into someone else's mould. It's time to celebrate being one of a kind! Nobody's personality will please everyone but living a life of integrity and self-belief will never go out of style.

"*Embrace Integrity* and *Self-Belief.*"

"Celebrate Imperfections!"

In a world full of glossy celebrity photos and social media posts, it's easy to lose focus on what is real. Remember, a curated version of someone's life is not their whole story – it's the individual imperfections that we recognise in one another which bring variety and fun into our lives.

We've all got something we don't like about
ourselves because it makes us feel 'different'.
But wouldn't life be deathly dull if we were all
the same? Our differences make the world the
fascinating, amazing, jumbled up place that it is,
which is something to be proud of!

"*Unique is Beautiful.*"

When I am with you my world is so bright,
I feel like nothing more is due,

"You Bring Sunshine & Light.

KATE SUMMERS

We constantly make connections with other people, but a special connection — one that shines so brightly it burns away the grey clouds — is rare. Once that bond is made with someone, hang on to it and cherish every moment.

Everyone has good in them, but some people really
deliver when it comes to lighting up the world. These
skills aren't just sprinkles – they're the extra scoop and
double cherry on top of a being a fabulous human.
Try to emulate their sparkle on the most vanilla-ish days!

Some people are plain ice cream, but most come with an

Extra Scoop and Sprinkles!

Ten Inspiring Books.

These books will remind you of the difference that a
single individual can make to the world.

1.   *I Am Malala* by Malala Yousafzai

2.   *Eat, Pray, Love* by Elizabeth Gilbert

3.   *A Street Cat Named Bob* by James Bowen

4.   *You are a Badass: How to Stop Doubting Your Greatness and Start Living an Awesome Life* by Jen Sincero

5.   *The Gifts of Imperfection* by Brené Brown

6.   *Untamed* by Glennon Doyle

7.   *Humans of New York* by Brandon Stanton

8.   *The Year of Yes* by Shonda Rhimes

9.   *Conversations With Myself* by Nelson Mandela

10. *The Boy, the Mole, the Fox and the Horse* by Charlie Mackesy

We accumulate people as we go through life, but true
friends are those who stick by us whatever the weather.
When we turn to them in an hour, week or year of
need, they're there, ready to take our hand – without
question. Be the friend who shows up for the storms,
as well as the sunshine.

"A Real Friend"

is one who walks in when the rest of the world walks out.

WALTER WINCHELL

The world is a "*Better Place*" with each of us in it.

Don't ever imagine that the world would carry on in the same way without all the wonderful humans that live in it. At the end of each day, think back to all those moments where one person made a difference. Those moments could be small or large – both are equally significant. Whether it's receiving a cheering smile or hearing an infectious laugh – these are the simple things that make life a little bit brighter!

Aim to be the friend who offers support
without judgement.

A friend is one who overlooks your broken fence and

" *Admires the Flowers in your Garden.* "

UNKNOWN

We each have the power

"to Create

Good."

When the world is whirling around us,
it can be hard not to feel insignificant.
Yes, we are each just one person among
billions, but we have the power to create
something good every day. Even a small
act of kindness, passed on from person to
person, creates an amazing
butterfly effect.

Affirmations ... to help you

"Shine Bright"

These affirmations will help us learn to live
from the heart. If we collectively shine our light
into the world, the universe has to respond!

- Become a force for positive change.

- Make a contribution to the world, no matter how small.

- Be focused on what is possible – and do it!

- Every small step is a giant leap when we work as a team.

- Nothing can dim the light that shines from within us.

- Embrace every new day.

- What each of us gives out, we will get back.

- Smile!

- Happiness is a mirror – go ahead and reflect it!

- Learn to live with what cannot be changed.

"*Shine*"

like the whole universe is yours.

RUMI

We all feel introspective at times, particularly in the winter months, but to feel the sunshine we must first unfurl our leaves. Look outwards into the wider world with positivity. It's surprising how much the universe will give if we open ourselves up to accepting its gifts.

Human beings are quick to focus on what they don't like about themselves, but sometimes it takes listening to someone else to make us understand why we are special. If we all trust what we hear, our light will shine even brighter.

When I look at you, I see an

"*Amazing, Beautiful Person*"

who has so much to offer the world.

BARRIE DAVENPORT

49

Make the world feel a
" *Safer Place* "
for someone.

Sometimes, it feels like everything is working against us
and that our path is a dark and lonely one. Just reach out
– it only takes one hand to make someone's
world feel safe again.

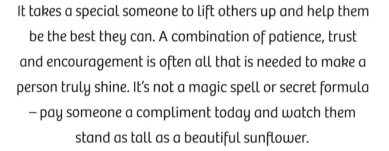

It takes a special someone to lift others up and help them be the best they can. A combination of patience, trust and encouragement is often all that is needed to make a person truly shine. It's not a magic spell or secret formula – pay someone a compliment today and watch them stand as tall as a beautiful sunflower.

"Bring out the Best in Everyone."

"*Anything*
is
Possible"

when you have the right people
there to support you.

MISTY COPELAND

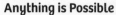

The people we spend our time with have a huge
influence on our mood, our view of the world
and the expectations we have of ourselves.
Choose these people well. They will inspire us,
but, importantly, they will challenge us. Then
anything really is possible!

Ten Empowering Films

Replace a self-help book with a movie night!
These uplifting films are perfect for inspiration and motivation.

- Pay it Forward (2000)
- The Pursuit of Happyness (2006)
- Yes Man (2008)
- Hidden Figures (2016)
- Of Mice and Men (1992)

- Life of Pi (2012)
- The Straight Story (1999)
- Good Will Hunting (1997)
- Into the Wild (2007)
- The Notebook (2004)

"Read All About it."

Recognising our achievements and giving ourselves a massive pat on the back for a job well done is an easy way to bring sunshine into a dull day. Make a list of small successes – even if it's just getting to the end of the week without incident! – and read it for a mood boost when doubt creeps in.

"Friends Are Those Rare People"

who ask how we are and then wait to hear the answer.

ED CUNNINGHAM

It takes a good friend to ask, "How are you?" and then really listen to what we have to say. They provide the space to open up and express our concerns when things aren't fine. Let them in if they offer support, and if everything is okay, enjoy sharing in each other's happiness.

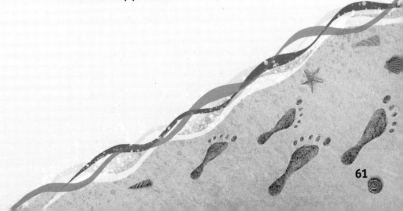

Everyone needs

"*Someone*

Who Shines."

We all have someone in our lives we can't
imagine being without. Perhaps they are
the one who understands us most, or a role
model who inspires and motivates us.
Each of us can be that person, we just need to
push any self-doubt firmly into the shadows
where it belongs.

We know that smiling is infectious, so spread it around!
The more we add to our bank of good deeds and
memories, the more we will have to smile about.
Before bed, try to think good thoughts. Write down three
positive acts to carry out the next day that will make
everyone feel happy.

"If you have good thoughts they will shine out of your face like sunbeams and

"You Will Always Look Lovely."

ROALD DAHL

Affirmations ... for

"Generating Sunshine"

When giving so much to others, we mustn't forget to look after our own physical and emotional well-being. These affirmations will help recharge the flattest of batteries.

- All is well in this moment in time.

- One minute, one hour, one day at a time.

- Everyone is doing their best – and that's usually enough.

- When times are testing, just breathe.

- Don't let little setbacks derail the whole day.

- Learning from challenges is a sign of growth.

- Never feel guilty about taking a moment to think.

- We all have the ability to achieve our dreams.

- Always anticipate the best from the day ahead.

- Anything may be possible even if everything isn't.

When times are challenging, never lose hope. The new dawn
shines brightest once the clouds finally part.

"Always Look for that Silver Lining."

"Your Crown"

has been bought and paid for.
Put it on your head and wear it.

MAYA ANGELOU

Most people find it hard to boast about doing something
well, but there's no harm in acknowledging success
or doing something that others might find inspiring.
Celebrate every achievement and wear that well-earned
crown with pride!

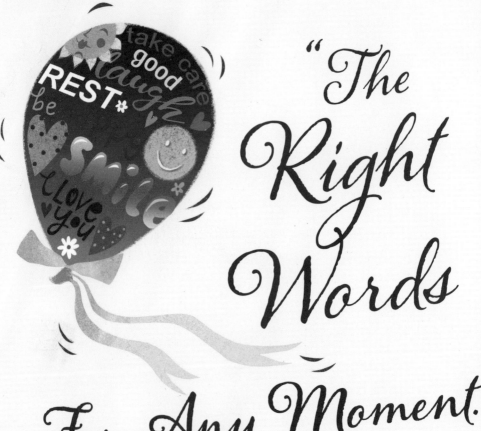

"The Right Words For Any Moment."

Knowing what to say at a difficult moment is something we can all struggle with. Often, it's better to remain quiet and just be there for the other person. If finding the right words comes naturally, say them and trust that they will bring comfort and hope.

Some people look for
a beautiful place.

"Others make
a Place
Beautiful."

HAZRAT INAYAT KHAN

Making every day feel special is a gift – let's celebrate those people who lift us up! Send a thank you note to someone who has delivered unexpected sunshine and spread the love.

"Small Actions, Big Impact."

Each of our unconscious
actions can make a difference
to someone else. A simple smile
or 'Thank you' can turn the day
around for a person who might
feel overlooked. Don't feel frustrated
by not visibly changing the world –
everyone leaves a mark just by being
their best self.

Some people are so much "*Sunshine* to the *Square Inch.*"

WALT WHITMAN

The people with the best
'sunshine-to-mainstream-human-qualities'
ratio are usually the ones who don't even realise it.
Humble, modest and quietly reassuring – these are the
characteristics that create a sense of security and peace
in others. Aspire to be the person who brings the warmth
to everyone around them!

Ten energy-raising
Songs!

Music has the power to boost our energy. We don't think about why it makes us feel uplifted, we just know it does. These feel-good songs will get everyone's good vibrations resonating!

- Walking on Sunshine – Katrina and the Waves

- Suddenly I See – KT Tunstall

- Lovely Day – Bill Withers

- Happy – Pharrell Williams

- Don't Worry, Be Happy – Bobby McFerrin

- Good Vibrations – Beach Boys

- I'm So Excited – The Pointer Sisters

- Here Comes the Sun – The Beatles

- You Are My Sunshine – Jimmie Davis

- Don't Stop Me Now – Queen

"Avoid
Unnecessary
Comparisons."

Comparing ourselves to other people can derail the best laid plans. Each of us is on our own journey and should never let unnecessary comparisons crush individual dreams.

Humans aren't made to exist in isolation. The true essence
of life comes through the connections we make and the
relationships that grow out of them. It is far better to have
a handful of close, supportive relationships than a hundred
that provide no nourishment at all.

To feel the love of people whom we love is a "*Fire that Feeds Our Life.*" ♥♥

PABLO NERUDA

"Live a Life Full of Gratitude."

Gratitude teaches us how to count our blessings and say 'Thank you' for the lovely things in our lives. It shines a light on the positives, restores our sense of perspective and allows us to make room in our hearts and lives to receive more of it. Take a moment every day to thank the universe for our most life-affirming experiences!

Each of us earns the love and trust of others simply by
being the best version of ourselves.

For the world, you can be one person, but for me,

" You Are the World. "

BRANDI SNYDER

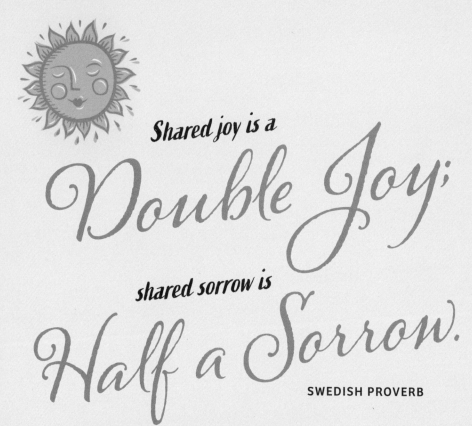

Shared joy is a

Double Joy;

shared sorrow is

Half a Sorrow.

SWEDISH PROVERB

By being present in other people's lives and sharing their emotions, we each help them in many ways. Our joy for them amplifies their own joy; our empathy makes any sadness that rests on their shoulders feel more manageable. Keep on bringing the sunshine when they need it.

An uninterrupted 30 minutes on the sofa with a good book, or an afternoon indulging in a favourite hobby, is sometimes exactly what we need to charge up our energy levels. Taking any opportunity to regroup in an increasingly hectic world is a valuable skill, so grab those moments whenever they arise!

Relax to
"Recharge".

Affirmations ... to end the day

Positively.

Bedtime affirmations bring a positive and calm end to the day
and cultivate empowering beliefs.

Take a few moments to repeat these before switching off the light.

- Rest happens when the mind is still.

- With each inhale, comes peace.

- With each exhale, tension departs.

- Thank you, world, for today's positive moments.

- A peaceful night is a reward for a productive day.

- Take solace in the moments when the world is calm.

- Seize the restorative power of sleep.

- Without moonlight, there can be no sunshine.

- Reflect, recover, regroup.

- Tomorrow is another opportunity to spread positivity.

A Final Thought...

If we all spread a little positivity every day, everyone's
world will become a better place.